Little Big Rooms

**New Nurseries
and Rooms to Play In**

gestalten

The First Four Walls

**by Interior Designer
Antonius Schimmelbusch**

Have you ever stepped on a Lego brick? Then you know: first, it hurts something awful, and second, nothing changes life in a household as much as when it is suddenly populated by children. Even if their arrival does not mean moving to a larger apartment or house, existing layouts are usually reconsidered—particularly in cities, where living space is becoming ever scarcer. Workrooms, dressing rooms, or other areas used for luxurious purposes then become children's rooms, which new parents set up with immense creative drive.

At no other point in history have children received as much attention as today. Contemporary parents devote a lion's share of their time to thinking about what is best for their children. This has long since included questions of style as well. On the Internet, innumerable blogs deal with childhood and its various manifestations in the form of interiors, playthings, and rituals. It is possible to state very clearly: childhood has become

"stylish." Discerning parents curate it visually.

And yet, our experience as an interior design duo, as designers of numerous children's rooms, and as mothers of a total of three children has taught us one thing above all: regardless of how much

> At no other point in history have children received as much attention as today.

pedagogical care and aesthetic ambition we employ in setting up rooms for our children—the most beautiful moments occur when the uninhibited creativity of the little ones manifests in places at home that originally had a very different function. When trains drive through tunnels made from chair legs, when stacks of books become shops, when music is

made on pots, and kitchen drawers serve as cozy dollhouses.

Or when, in the early hours of the morning, painting is not done on paper, but instead directly on top of the desk itself, giving rise to a felt-tip fantasy world so detailed and beautiful that a mother refrains from reproaching the child out of astonishment and pride. Or, when you at some point simply accept that opulent toy landscapes sometimes spread out in an otherwise rigorously minimalist living room, and that you have to share a bathtub not only with a child, but also with what seems like 100 Schleich animals.

At such moments, the boundaries between the children's room and what is allowed have long since blurred. The planned and the regulated, which we as parents so frequently try to establish, gives way to the spontaneous, to the chaos that arises from the euphoria of the moment.

As designers, we naturally do not want, for instance, to spread the message that you should let chaos take its course. ▶

The most beautiful thing about living with children is that we are allowed to become children again ourselves.

▼ We ourselves instead try every day to channel the chaos that our children cause. Thus, what interests us when setting up a room is creating spatial situations that give children a feeling of security and also stimulate their imaginations; having children learn a sense of order, but not limiting their creativity; getting them used to the ritual of sharing with siblings or friends; and, yes, teaching them something like pride of ownership as well.

Understanding a child's personality is also always important. And so we try to coax the optimal stimulation—for the specific young individual who lives in it—out of a children's room. When a four-year-old boy still always has an irrepressible urge to move after long days at daycare, wall bars with a soft gym mat where he is able to let off steam can perhaps help. If a child is dreamy, often leaves his

or her possessions lying around, and still has trouble getting organized, then the child needs, all the more, a room with a clear and simply manageable organization system.

When two siblings share a room and constantly fight about everything, a strict (we recommend colorful) division of all work, play, and storage areas into "mine" and "yours" helps. When a child, on the other hand, develops a great passion for reading, an inviting and comfortable reading corner, with light playing a central role, can encourage this passion.

When one has a desire to design, this question naturally arises: For whom are we parents now setting up the room—for the child or for ourselves? In response, we encourage egoism. When a comfortable adult armchair, with space for one and half people, is situated in the children's room, you will surely prefer to read books together there, rather than sitting on the floor, hunching over the bed, or otherwise being reduced to munchkin format. The most beautiful thing about living with children is that we are allowed to become children again ourselves. ●

◀ Team Antonius Schimmelbusch
Interior Design: Melissa Antonius
and Lena Schimmelbusch (left)

Little Conquerors

How Adults Can Defend Their Territory

A Brio train runs through the living room, a bassinet stands in the parents' bedroom, and a toddler makes noise on a miniature-format wooden stove in the kitchen. This is a scenario that all parents can identify with: children are suddenly everywhere—and if not the children themselves, then their colorful traces of odds and ends. Children like to make the entire home their territory, and not only when their own rooms are small.

It is a positive thing when children develop an imagination and are permitted to implement their ideas at home, especially since it is seldom possible to simply send them out into the city alone. Children should, however, still learn that: there is adult territory that I may only use to a limited extent—and only with permission—and there is my territory, where I can do as I please, as long as I tidy up again later.

If corners for children are firmly installed in spaces for adults—for instance a play kitchen (there are beautiful models by Brio or Djeco) in the real kitchen, or a table for arts and crafts (for ▶

▲ Whether the cause is a lack of space or a desire for closeness—the fact is that a baby crib often stands in the parents' bedroom. It's wonderful when it, as here, fits into the color canon of the room. The curtain provides protection against bright light.

▶ Harry Potter would be jealous: a reading niche has been created for the children in this open living room of a loft apartment. A foam mattress, a couple of pillows, and, naturally, a reading lamp create a cozy place to withdraw in a simple way.

▼ example by Richard Lampert) and/or a reading corner in the living room—such areas should always have enough boxes, drawers, or baskets in which the little conquerors can quickly stow away their playthings after use. If parents encounter resistance in connection with tidying up, we recommend threatening children with the vacuum-cleaner scenario: if it

children are suddenly everywhere with their colorful traces of odds and ends.

comes out, everything will be gone afterward.

People who like rugs can easily share them with their children in the living room, also because flooring made of natural materials is much more robust than one might think. In this case, we advise: do not select an infantile pattern, but instead take the rest of the furnishings as a guide when choosing a ▶

▲ With blackboard paint, it is possible to visually mark off a play area in the living room and to provide space for all kinds of doodles—perhaps by parents as well.

Upper right: A campsite in the living room is a temporary pleasure that gives children maximum enjoyment in the short term and can also disappear quickly again.

▶ Intergenerational use: in this workroom, it is also possible to build at will. When adults need free tabletops, the playthings can quickly disappear into crates once again.

▼ A win-win situation: children particularly like to cook in their own mini-kitchen, positioned in their parents' kitchen. This model from IKEA has been slightly modified and given more storage space. The chair is for parents who would like to taste the results.

▶ This mobile crib by RatzRaum (available from Afilii) is ideal for the early phase: when the nursery is not yet being used, the baby can be put down to sleep wherever it is most convenient, for instance, in the room of older siblings when the television is not on, or, if the baby likes to hear voices, next to the dining table.

Bottom right: Children love high seats and step stools. These variants are available from Afilii and make it possible for children to always be involved and observe things—whether when cooking or when brushing their teeth at their parents' sink.

▼rug. The new softness on the floor is invitation enough for children to spend hours there reading, playing, or merely sprawling around. Infants who are just discovering their fine motor skills particularly enjoy rolling around on carpet, staring at patterns, touching the structure with their fingers, and rolling over for the first time—in the best case with naked legs. Especially at the beginning, it is necessary to take babies along into nearly every room, and rugs, baby swings, or bassinets with wheels are suitable, temporary aids that can disappear again later on. For birthday celebrations, tents and canopies are a highlight that can be set up in the living or dining room short term. Cam Cam Copenhagen and bobo kids offer particularly good models. If this ritual is repeated every year, such small installations always remain fascinating and become imprinted for life as special birthday landscapes.

And a little tip for hot summer days as well: if there is no garden or balcony, a mini-pool (it can also be the baby bathtub), in which a child can splash around, is a good option. ●

Laurence Dougier

▲ Designer Laurence Dougier and architect Emmanuel Dougier turned a derelict paper factory outside Paris into a bohemian fantasy. Atop a wooden stair, their daughters' bedrooms seem to be in the belly of an old Spanish galleon, with decorative masks and one pair of cherub's wings hanging from the balustrade.

▶ The sheets are clean and soft (H&M duvet cover, La Redoute bed), even the toys are stored inside toys (Lego boxes), and no matter how far you wander, you'll always find your way home again (poster by Famille Summerbelle). And after every rain, there is a rainbow (cloud mobile by The Butter Flying).

The Colors of Life

Full of character, layered, and unified by a subdued but cheerful color scheme, the Project R home by Avenue Lifestyle includes a playroom and the daughters' bedroom. Playroom cabinets are painted in Farrow & Ball's Elephant's Breath, while the walls are warm, youthful, and feminine in Dead Salmon. The women added linen roman blinds, vintage chairs, bunting flags, IKEA storage boxes, the girls' own artwork, and ordinary two-by-fours to create a floor-to-ceiling screen. The bedroom features half-painted walls, cushy linens, a Moroccan-style rug, and a princess's palette, like that of the playroom downstairs. ●

A Room of One's Own

Just a few well-chosen pieces can turn an ordinary room into a snuggly nursery and, in this day and age, they're pieces that anyone can find. This space looks elegant enough for grown-up entertaining—with its sleek furnishings, shades of gray, and range of textures—but it's also scaled perfectly to little tots. A bunny lamp and a woolly, charcoal gray rocking sheep live in a landscape grown by IKEA, including a Strandmon wing chair and a laminated birch play kitchen (complete with induction range), under the diffuse, warm light of the pink, crinkled-textile Hemsta light shade. ●

Past Renewed

▲ Two little girls dream and play in a bedroom that combines old and new. In their central Malmö apartment, stylist and Miloii shop owner Karolina Vertus and her carpenter husband Daniel Magnusson mix modern natural materials with antiques, flea market finds, and Bohemian textures for their daughters.

TECHNĒ ARCHITECTURE + INTERIOR DESIGN

Color Garden

Technē Architecture + Interior Design preserved a neoclassically columned fireplace, lending this otherwise contemporary bedroom a cozy classicism. The prevalence of white, except for a coffee-color rug, makes color and texture pop onto the eyes: a circular area rug made of multicolored pom-poms, a vivid purple felt sculpture, an elephant duvet, a dollhouse with pink window trim and green shrubbery, two color-lined white boxes, framing a piggy bank and an owl, mounted above the bed. Another owl looks out from a bookshelf across the room. ●

▲ Midnight blue walls against the white skirting and wooden floors creates a neutral color scheme in shared bedrooms. The emphasis is on creating a communal space for the siblings to dance, read and play together. Furniture like the Milimboo cabinet can hold and display the children's toys and games.

Sigmar London

▶ Axel's bedroom is tucked into an eighteenth-century lakeside Swedish farmhouse made bright and practical by designer Sigmar London. He equipped the room with underbed storage, a circus tent, and a mountaineering monkey hanging from the wall, while angled wall sections provide a cozy sense of shelter.

Fabienne
Collombel

▶ A room analogous to a mixed bouquet in a simple vase: in Marseille, the designer Fabienne Collombel adorned white walls with flecks of bright colors: a sprawling floral wall sticker, a flowered pink Japanese paper lantern, a pink-petaled Smila Blomma IKEA wall lamp, polka-dotted bed linens, and a candy-colored rug.

Josh Schweitzer

▲ In this children's bedroom in Los Angeles, California, Josh Schweitzer combined matte turmeric yellow and glossy sky blue, while exploiting large windows on the ground floor that look out onto lush greenery. To make the most of a small space, he built a sprawling chest of drawers into the base of the single bed.

STUDIO REVOLUTION

Beach Scene

In this Bolinas, California, beach house and holiday home for a family of four, Studio Revolution created a nursery and guest room from a diminutive attic space with a low, four-foot doorway. The studio used sand-colored carpet, a Stone pouf by Five Times One, and raindrop decals that fall down two walls. The crib was placed in one of the three closets. An Eames LCW chair, a cowhide from Pure Rugs, and a Miffy lamp round out the furniture, while the finishes—Benjamin Moore Super White walls and Mopboard Black window and door accents—echo the rest of the house's modern finishes. ●

Retro Roommates

▼ Old school modernity? Architect, interior, and furniture designer Julia von Werz's London home represents a mash-up of British townhouse and vintage treasures discovered in Munich. Under the roof, she populated the playroom with toys like an antique wicker perambulator and a dollhouse-size grocery store.

KARINA KALIWODA

Living Together

A former fashion designer, who now consults on home improvement, created a play corner for her son in a corner of her Hamburg living room instead of separating the baby from the rest of the house. She mixed affordable products from IKEA, H&M, and HEMA (storage boxes, a larger-than-life Cloud lamp, and play carpet) with flea-market finds (doll pram, vintage chair, wooden tractor) and retro pieces like a toy car. A gray canopy and star-shaped cushions from Numero 74 form a little man-cave. From the nubbly felt Sukhi carpet to the crocheted mobile from DaWanda, everything is as soft as the baby's skin. ●

Let There Be Light!

Light, Dark, "Not Quite Dark"

▲ Corresponding to the playful look of this room, a hot-air balloon floats over the bed—replacing a bedside light here as a result of its low mounting.

◀ In this colorful children's room, the focus is on a strong trio of ceiling lamps. In the evening, a desk lamp brings light into the darkness.

It is a tremendous moment when a child's hand reaches the light switch for the first time. Previously, light and dark were firmly in the parents' hands—but the child is now able to banish the darkness his- or herself.

A child's room is at times a precision workshop, other times a cave. Sometimes, sophisticated Lego landscapes are created in it over several days, erected under almost clinical lighting, then a rope is once again spanned through the room to create a tent landscape with all the blankets available in the household, from which only the weak light of a child's flashlight flickers.

Different activities require different lighting solutions. However, the basis has to be a bright ceiling lamp with sufficient light diffusion. Like daylight, it promotes concentration and is ideal for finding missing doll shoes or for tidying up. Our own childhood was shaped by IKEA's Noguchi, the delicate rice-paper balloon. Today, there are no longer any limits to the imagination: hot-air balloons (for example by Cam Cam Copenhagen) float over the center of the room; or suns, moons, and sometimes even ▶

Different activities require different lighting solutions.

▼ clouds, which are simultaneously loudspeakers (for instance by Richard Clarkson), hang over the realm of little people.

To facilitate various atmospheres, we divide the room into different areas. So there may be, for instance, a corner for work, where arts and crafts are made and homework is later done. A desk is put in the best possible light with a table lamp—with light ideally coming from the left for right-handed children, and from the right for left-handers.

A standing lamp, on the other hand, immerses a comfortable armchair, a sofa, or even just a pile of pillows in a cozy cone of light—ideal for reading (together). Standing lamps are, however, not suitable for small children, because not only the children but also the lamp might fall over during play; so for starters, it's preferable to use a low-hanging ceiling lamp. The light should generally come from at least three different sources so as to illuminate the room evenly.

The wonderful thing about children's rooms: strings of lights are always in season! Wound around the headboard of the

▲ Children's book heroes are ideal night watchmen—as, in this case, "Miffy" the bunny (from Mr Maria), which was invented in the Netherlands in 1955.

▶ In addition to basic and zone lighting, the accent lighting is a quite subtle and decorative light source—here in the form of an applique. Such appliques come into their own on colorful walls in particular.

◀ Strings of lights are always in season in children's rooms and set colorful accents.

▼ The glass "Memory" air balloons from Brokis hang under the ceiling of this children's room as if filled with helium and provide atmospheric basic lighting.

bed or through the room as a garland, such light sources (for instance by Mimi'lou) set magical accents. In the case of young children, strings of lights have to be mounted out of reach or, when in doubt, foregone completely. Illuminated figures (with LEDs, because they do not get hot, but, if possible, ones made of plastic without BPA and softening agents) are one alternative, since they provide charm and a mellow shimmer of light and can also serve as a magical night-light (for example by Egmont Toys or A Little Lovely Company). ●

▼ Sleep like big people! Like a master bedroom, this children's room has been streamlined for symmetry. The vibrant red bases of the ceramic lamps look like fat balloons.

▲ A sky full of rice-paper balloons makes this reading corner unique. A table lamp with an owl base immerses the chair in softer light as needed.

Top left: In 80 days around the world—with the hot-air balloon made of rice paper with a textile cable from Cam Cam Copenhagen, every child becomes a globetrotter.

◀ A place to cuddle: the dimmable "Brown Bear" lamp from Mr Maria provides a cozy light source with a twist of the hand.

Romantic Romp

There's no need to be afraid of the dark. This dreamy bedroom is enchanted by tapestry-like wallpaper—a reproduction of William Morris's Strawberry Thief pattern from 1883—featuring an elaborate pattern on a black ground. Like the romantic bed canopy, which recalls knights, damsels, and the quest for Camelot, it should help to conjure sweet dreams. Beneath original ornate ceiling moldings, the pink-nosed Heico/Egmont Bunny Rabbit lamp is as charming switched off as it is warm and comforting when turned on. ●

Oliver Burns

▼ The children's room in Oliver Burns's rural Bedfordshire, England, home is painted in pale hues, but it is kinetically colorful, too. Small fields of red and flecks of navy—a scarlet desk lamp, drapery cornices, a bouquet of balloon ceiling lights, chevron-pattern Roman shades—give the room a hot energy.

The Four Walls

Striped, Spotted, Individual

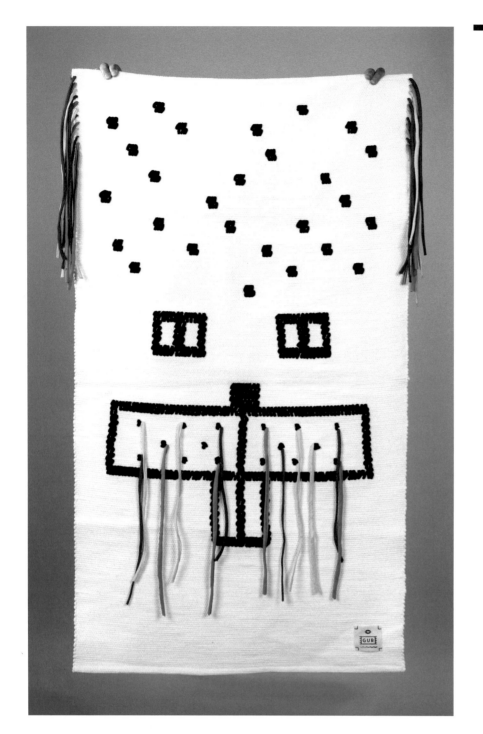

▲ The wall hangings from GUR are produced on order. This one was designed by the Spanish illustrator José Ja Ja Ja.

▶ More is more! The Castanea floral carpet from House of Hackney sets the tone in this room. The simple loft bed from Oliver Furniture and the graphic bed linens provide a contrast.

N o room changes as rapidly as a child's room. Each phase has its particular challenges, each age its heroes. Create a framework that adapts to your child's shifting preferences! Age-related motifs such as Smurfs, ice princesses, or Minions should only appear on objects that can be exchanged quickly and, if possible, inexpensively—for instance on bed linens or posters.

Wallpaper, curtains, and carpet or rugs should, however, be more long-lasting—but this does not necessarily mean that the color spectrum has to be reduced to white and beige hues. We like using colors and patterns in children's rooms as a targeted accent: for instance, ▶

Each phase has its particular challenges, each age its heroes.

▼ wallpapering one wall instead of all of them—which achieves a refined rather than cluttered look. We recommend that novices, when it comes to color, only use the color desired (by the child) up to a height of around 90 centimeters. Doing so frames the room in a panel-like way and leaves space above for lighter shades.

Is your child passionate about the film *Moana*? Why not apply wallpaper with a leaf motif on the wall behind the bed (for example Palmeral from House of Hackney), which will be able to outlast the Hawaiian trend? Or does your son dream of pirates? When applied to one wall or even the ceiling, Midnatt from Sandberg can give rise to an adventure scenario. And the dark-blue waves are then also still cool when your child has long since abandoned his pirate flags.

For people who still find all of this too permanent, we can recommend wall stickers. It is usually possible to remove them easily and satisfy your child's preferences in real time (we discovered particularly flamboyant stickers at Studio Ditte). Or follow the advice of the style icon Diana Vreeland

▲ A world as we like it: granny-style floral wallpaper comes together with furniture that we know and love from Pippi Longstocking's Villa Villekulla.

▶ A real winner: a carpet that can also be used as a racetrack!

and hang a horizon-expanding world map in you child's room (for instance from Lilipinso).

However, not only the walls (and the ceiling) offer design possibilities—the floor also has potential. Here, achieving an interplay between hard and soft areas is ideal. On wood or linoleum (available in many colors from Forbo and DLW Flooring), it is easy for cars and trains to roll, and small figures are able to stand stably on such surfaces. At the same time, if you lay a soft rug on the floor, it can take up the color concept, depict your child's favorite animal, ▶

▲ The magnetic wallpapers from Sian Zeng are magical and engage young and old.

▼ 3D, recycled cardbaord turned to decoration by Studio ROOF who centre their work around imagination, play and craftsmanship.

or serve as an island of calm in the tempestuous ocean of playthings. And so that it is also possible to play on the rug, we recommend short-pile varieties.

Colors and patterns can even ensure tranquility and peace—namely, when siblings share a room. A color code for the walls behind the beds or desks (or on baskets, drawers, bed linens, etc.), developed in cooperation with your children, can stake out their territories decoratively and helps to design children's coexistence more harmoniously. ●

▲ Mounted on the wall, a collection of vintage playthings, children's chairs, and display cases is a real eye-catcher.

▶ Mirrors, frames, and vacation souvenirs from family trips can also provide diverse decorations in children's rooms.

▶▶ People who find wallpaper or striking colors on the wall to be too much can satisfy their children's creative desires with wall stickers.

▲ Cabin magic: this room has been given a vacation mood by means of inexpensive plywood paneling. A pennant and small shelves that provide space for cherished playthings do the rest.

▶ Are four colorful walls too bold for you? Then set a targeted accent and decide for one wall. Tip: involve your child in the decision—the result will surprise you.

◀ Entire worlds can be created with wallpaper, as here with plants and the wallpaper for Jungle Book fans from Sian Zeng.

EMILIE MUNROE

Shared Space

Life can go a little "bananas" when you're raising little humans. When Emilie Munroe of San Francisco's Studio Monroe was pregnant, she took her own excellent advice, incorporating her own aesthetic into the baby's nursery, because they were about to start spending a lot of time there. Munroe paired cheerful colors—turquoise walls, a yellow rocker—with natural wood and rattan furniture, featuring no sharp edges beyond the rug's diamond pattern. She finished with the b-a-n-a-n-a-s! wall covering from Flavor Paper, the Elephant Dresser from Pottery Barn Kids, a Blu Dot pendant light, and The Container Store baskets. ●

Seriously Childish

This playland welcomes kids with 1980s vintage Inspector Gadget and E.T. The owner of the children's fashion label Arsene et Les Pipelettes designed her own family's Basque country home. Mixes of colors and patterns—a rainbow rug, children's drawings—with fields of white and materials ranging from brass to cushy upholstery invite use with their energy, softness, and contrasts. In the children's rooms, unused toys are stored in Pop-Line boxes under the bed or displayed on a vintage school-desk-like table with chairs. ●

Ros Walshe

▼ Old objects tell new stories in new contexts. Ros Walshe decorated this children's playroom in Ireland with sage-green walls and an eclectic mix of antique and vintage toys: eighteenth-century Scandinavian chairs, life-size push-toy dogs, and, mounted to the wall, a children's chair and a bouquet of black ice skates.

Into the Wild

Go "wild" with your decor—and your
imagination—to compliment the
simplicity of this black-and-white jungle
mural. Printed on non-woven
wallpaper by the Paris textile design
studio and shop Bien Fait, which
celebrates the manual genius of French
artisans, The Wild was inspired by artist
Henri Rousseau's landscape work. ●

Embracing a Hue

Give your child a room that hugs them. This interior features sweet details and a 360° use of color, a mesmerizing hue that anticipates the sky before dusk in summer (try the similar Totally Tony by designer Anna von Mangoldt). The Kids Concept chair and table by Pirum add a little stardust to the high-ceilinged space, while the Rocking Sheep by Danish Crafts updates the traditional rocking horse. Carved by hand from wood and clad in real lamb's wool, each has an encompassing shagginess that is inviting and unique. ●

JENNIFER YAMSEK

A Bookworm's World

In an age of maximalism, more is more and clutter is creative. And where better to live with more than in a child's bedroom? Illustrator and book blogger Jennifer Yamsek, based in Atlanta, Georgia, turned toys and books into interior design elements for her little ones. Here, books play a prominent role but live side by side with the characters in them—on Kukkia bookshelves shaped like gabled houses. The white walls of the bedroom disappear behind the room's contents, just as, in the imagination, the pages of a book disappear behind the words on the page. ●

Parisean

Keep telling stories even when the books are closed: the planet- and people-friendly Atelier Choux carrés are artful and artisanal bibs and bed linens, wall stickers, cushions, and even packaging shaped as a hôtel particulier—lyrically hand-drawn by Swedish illustrator Mattias Adolfsson. As collectible artworks made in an eco-certified factory and printed on an organic cotton weave, each drawing tells a whimsical story—pastel-hued, humorous, fantastical: steampunk airships, intricate architecture, puffy white clouds with chubby faces, even hot-air balloons decorated like birthday cakes. ●

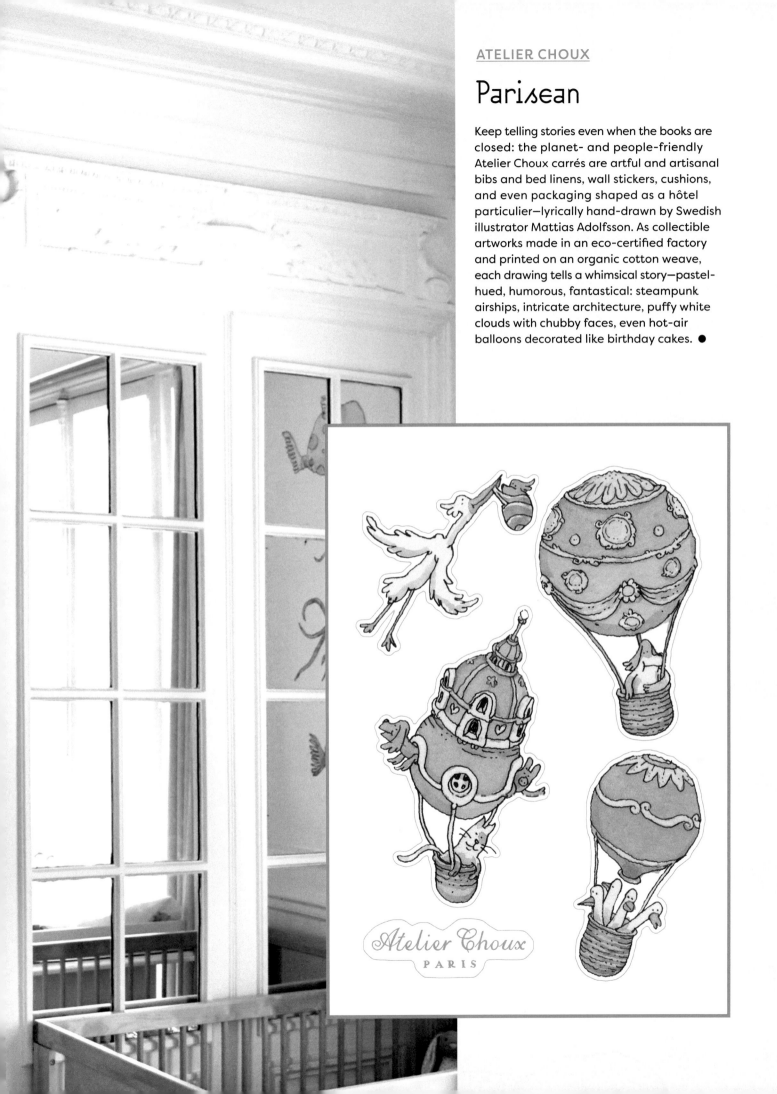

SIAN ZENG

Illustrated Interiors

A Central Saint Martins graduate and young-talent-to-watch, London-based Zeng brings her own dreams to work with her. Pairing advanced technologies with traditional techniques, she creates storybook surfaces that wrap—and enchant—walls, cushions, sofas, and more. Her sofa.com collaboration includes fabric by the meter, a sofa, armchair, footstool, and blanket box. The furniture features waterdrop-shaped wooden limbs, while Zeng's Woodlands wallpaper depicts hedgehogs and frogs, tiny trees, and houses beside oversize flowers, in unconventional colorways like brown/pink and khaki/blue. ●

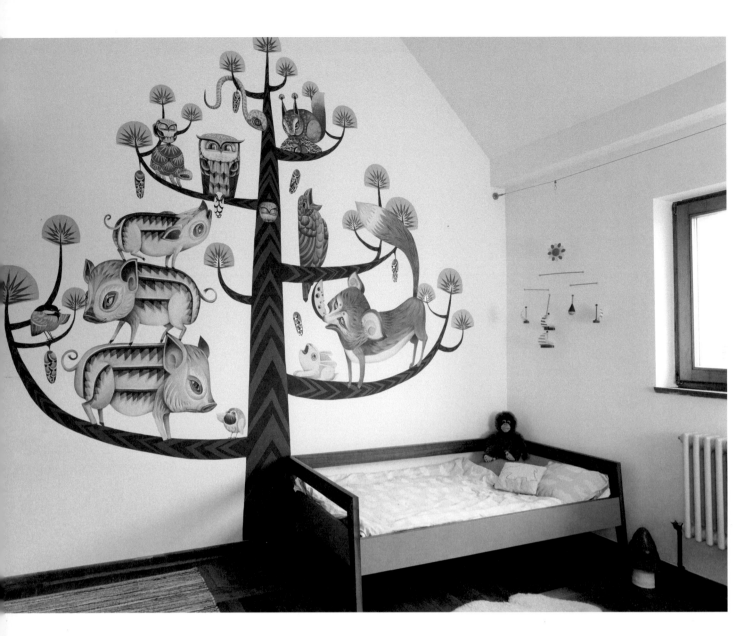

POLINA
SOLOVEICHIK

Magical Murals

Turn your children's bedroom walls into windows overlooking dreamlands. Russia-born, Berlin-based artist Polina Soloveichik began her career painting on New York City streets, learning to integrate her artwork completely into its context. Raising two children, Soloveichik witnessed "the dreamy reality and the real dreams" in which kids live. Each mural is hand-painted and bespoke to both child and room: a tokay gecko smiles down from the ceiling, a whale dances with jellyfishes, and in a corner there is a daydreaming elfin girl and a mother monkey embracing her baby with that deepest of all loves. ●

Practical Magic

Strike a balance of organic-industrial and adult-child in bedroom decor. In this room, blond wood and natural throws mix with a steel table lamp and a white Eames DSW chair for toddler and infant. The neutral colors have depth while the bassinet, in lightweight rattan, provides texture and can be easily carried to different parts of the house or even outside. Above the bed, a fairyland garland of Cotton Ball Lights by WestwingNow makes a practical room just a bit enchanted. ●

ANNA LANDSTEDT

A Warm Northern Glow

Pewter, cinnamon, milk white: in this nursery, Landstedt again invokes a swank Scandinavian sensibility. Here, organic materials—cotton, blond-wood toys—are accompanied by a warm, spicy palette. The space will transform into a toddler's room as the baby grows: the changing table from Ollie|s|Out converts into a dresser and the Sebra crib will become a bed. Landstedt painted the lower walls light brown, hung garlands by Atelier Sukha from the ceiling, and deepened the cozy quotient with a Moroccan-style carpet by Ellos and a fabric canopy by Numero 74 that glows above the crib. ●

Dip-Dyed Desert Dreams

Eclectic, energetic, but not cluttered. The Netherlands' Live Loud Girl furnished this bohemian-inflected nursery with handcrafted White Moss Decor. Against gridded wallpaper, the wicker crib (dressed in lamb-soft blankets from Kate & Kate Home) is the room's focus—light and transparent. Splashes of color come from: Pinch toys cars and a Mikanu pear, a Lamia Beni Ourain Moroccan rug handwoven by Berber women from Maison Saadah, a rattan mirror and IKEA hanging shelves spray-painted green, and wall-mounted masks. The curtains? A simple DIY project, dipped partially in orange dye. ●

Structured Play

Under the steep angle of a gabled roof and a tall skylight, the designer has exposed the topmost wooden beams of the building and painted an exposed pipe black, emphasizing architectural structure like another plaything. A few subdued patterns pop out of predominantly white surfaces: Ferm Living's Harlequin wallpaper in mint and an area rug in a gray scalloped pattern. A bear-faced storage bag can be used to hold either clothes or toys, while Nubie's Wild & Soft Plush Lion Head adds to the room's plush playfulness. ●

Light & Bright

As a parent, you're going to clean them regularly anyway, so dare to paint interior surfaces blank paper white—especially when you're decorating interiors inside a rustic or industrial building. In this old structure, the designer exposed its brick and wood-beam skeleton while whitewashing walls and timber-plank floors and ceilings to give the room a bright airiness. White surfaces frame a Wild & Soft Plush Lion Head and Tiger Head by Nubie above a vintage school desk and chair. ●

A Detailed Design

In this bright, white room, softness takes the form of a few easy DIY details: a life-size rabbit light lives beside a wooden Alexander Girard doll above a fluffy sheepskin rug. A pair of red Converse sneakers and a wooden guitar serve as wall art, while a tall Tellkiddo Paper Bag featuring a bear's face adds more character to the room. Along with two big woven baskets that soften the bold lines of the adjacent crib, it makes a perfect home for sock monkeys and other toys when not in use. ●

Out of Sight ...

Keeping, Storing, and Learning to Organize

Children seek out their own niches for rituals. They select new favorite locations again and again. And they are utterly fascinated by new objects time after time. It is usually not a fancy Steiff elephant chosen by the parent that becomes a favorite animal, but instead a ragged mongrel that the child obtained through swapping, or a ghastly neon cat from outer space with big round eyes. Children also frequently glorify quite simple things—for instance, a stone found on a walk, which is then given a painted face and carefully treasured in a bed fashioned from a matchbox, resting within view on the nightstand.

Children therefore need an organization system that already helps them deal with tidying up from a young age. This means, first of all, that there should be drawers or receptacles in their room which they are able to open and close on their own (simple and good: from IKEA or Flexa). This gives children a feeling of self-sufficiency within their own four walls.

Keeping an overview is also important: the best option is ▶

◀ The play furniture from CasieLiving is a combination of case and dollhouse, provides space for small items, and also becomes a pit stop with some tape on the floor.

▶ Designing spaces makes it easier to keep them tidy: this child-size wardrobe is constructed of sticks, while the forest is continued on the wall with Washi tape.

to give each type of plaything its own place: a windowsill for a growing collection of dinosaurs; a box for building blocks; a bookshelf suitable for children's books, which are often large-format, since stacks of books are usually hard for children to handle; a pinboard for artworks; a box for pencils and crayons.

For order in children's rooms—always a controversial issue between the generations—there are simple rules that can definitely be taught to children: only accumulate as many possessions as there is space available

▶ Nothing steps out of line here thanks to the animal coat hooks from ferm LIVING.

▼ A clothes rail with costumes is a wonderful alternative to a classic dress-up suitcase! The outfits are easily accessible and will therefore be used more often.

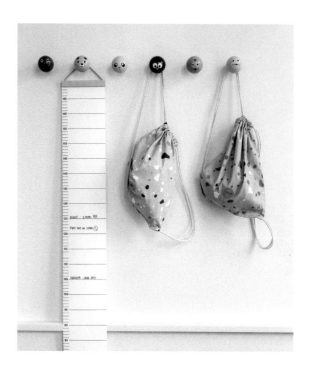

to stow them away. Playthings should therefore be passed along regularly—to younger siblings, friends, or people in need. Children enjoy parting with things and are willing to generously give things away as gifts if one explains to them that another child would enjoy a puzzle as well.

We also recommend tidying up together thoroughly once a month in order to return the room to the ideal state desired, where everything is stowed away in a truly optimal manner. This is the only way for a child to get used to this state of affairs and come to appreciate it at some point. It is perfectly understandable that this state will quickly vanish again, and that a child will not want to disassemble everything and put it away after playing. But a certain basic order that makes it possible to at least cross the room safely should be achieved in the evening. ▶

▼ In these simple as well as charming tepees from JULICA, there is space for books and play figurines—transitions between tidying up and playing are sometimes barely recognizable.

▶ The Harlequin bench from Cam Cam Copenhagen provides space for all kinds of playthings in children's rooms. In the hallway, it is a tried-and-tested place for storing and putting on shoes.

A few words about clothing—a separate topic—as well. Until children learn to dress themselves, their clothing should definitely be stored out of reach of their hands. Clothing is all too often spontaneously pulled out for playing and then disappears and/or ends up on stuffed animals and dolls. And there is no guarantee that it can be found when really needed. Most children are long overtaxed by "clothing regulations"—often, unfortunately, until they begin school; we cannot provide a more optimistic prognosis in this regard. ●

▲ Drawers under the bed and a metal cupboard ensure order in this room. The vintage look is timeless and will easily survive the leap from children's to teen bedroom.

▶ A room niche has here been made into an open closet. Identical hangers ensure a unified picture for colorful rows of clothing.

▲ Space found! In this old apartment, an inoperative fireplace serves as a book-shelf and exhibition space for cars, superheroes, and Co.

Top right: The changing table from the Harlequin series by Cam Cam Copenhagen provides space for all the necessities during the diaper-wearing phase and is a beautiful commode in the years afterward.

▶ The strong carpet pattern demands order. This is ensured in a playful way in this room by means of a spacious chest of drawers and a large trunk.

▶▶ This room does not forfeit its charming boho-character, despite the order. Playthings are arranged here in the open on surfaces or disappear into cases or baskets.

The Enchanted Forest

The enchantment of a magic forest with its fabulous flora and fauna has been translated into a children's room. In fact, this masterfully abstracted version of a bright fairy-tale forest is made entirely of IKEA products. Trees, moss, and ferns become cushions, bedding, and painted wooden crates in various shades of green. The bed transforms into a shed or lean-to. And the room—which is filled with neutral, clear surfaces and natural materials like wood, fabric, and paper—is also a Scandinavian-inflected environment that any grown-up can love. ●

ESPEN SURNEVIK

Family Living

The Norwegian architect Espen Surnevik built his three kids into the family's 1924 house, integrating their activities throughout instead of limiting them to a bed- or playroom. He backed the living room sofa with a kid-size desk and cut a "parking space" out of a wall of cabinets to store the kids' laminated wooden scooter. Gymnastics rings hang from the ceiling, and in the office-playroom toys form a mountainous island at the center, surrounded by a perimeter of the parents' flat files and binders. The bed is a long divan under floor-to-ceiling bookshelves accessed by a rolling ladder more typical of a classical library. ●

Fun-damental

Putting the "fun" into the functional: the young German design label JULICA combines minimal aesthetics with clever capabilities to create children's furniture and gifts, as well as home accessories. The designers say they "oppose dull mass products," strong words that are followed up by strong ideas: a blue whale holds books in its mouth or atop its head, and wooden Tipikids tepees can serve as magazine racks or to frame play space. A wall-mounted crocodile is both shelf and coatrack, the pastel Zookids stools are little elephants, lions, and hippos, and the play table can even become a fort. ●

Man & Machine

The joinery brand Müller Möbelwerkstätten has been making furniture since 1869—and yet its children's furniture is more modern than modern. Historical expertise, artisanry, and CNC capabilities create clever and formally sleek pieces. The Stacking bed was created in 1966 as a lounger by Rolf Heide, while the formally crisp and cartoonish Plane collection seems to have its origins in graphic design: a compact secretary, the outline of a house that is a playhouse for the imagination to fill in, and Boxit shelves, with crisp lines but radiused corners. ●

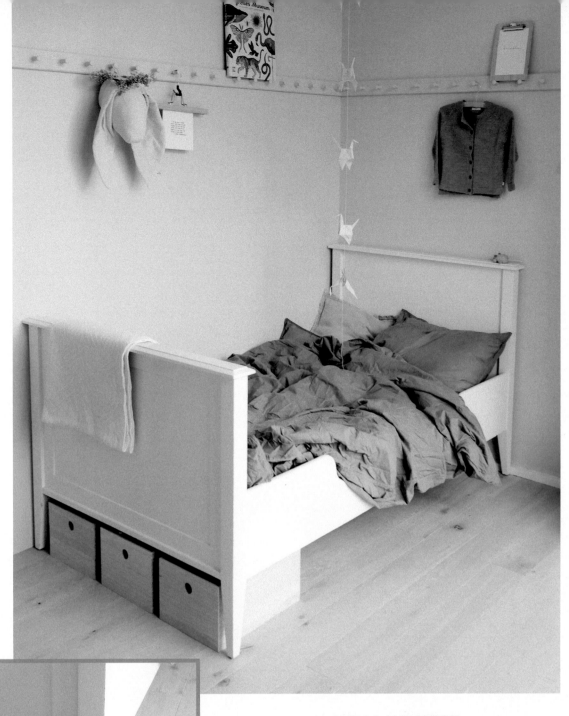

ANNA LANDSTEDT

Northern Nightlights

This toddler's bedroom is focused around light colors and natural materials like wood, cotton, and even straw. Landstedt organized toys in hemp baskets and hung toys, clothes, and art across a long, Shaker-style peg rack. Most brands and furniture are northern, including a Swedish Midnatt bed, paint colors by Nordsjö, a Danish karlekammerskab (or linen closet, used here as wardrobe), a desk and chair by the Danish brand Ferm Living, and bookshelves made from an IKEA spice rack. The gymnastics rings hanging from the ceiling are by the Finnish brand Lillagunga, one of the designer's children's room signatures. ●

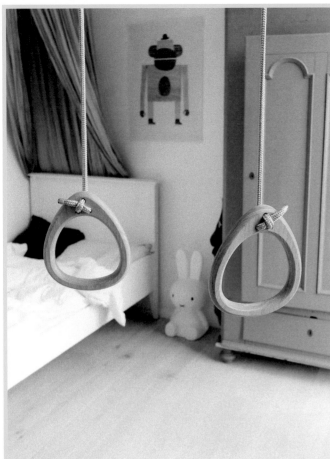

ANNA LANDSTEDT

Behind the Scenes

Like a theater's backstage—organized for quick changes but filled with costumes displayed on an IKEA coathanger and curiosities—this little boy's room is sophisticated and fun. It pairs minimal, modern living space with vintage Scandinavian wooden furniture, including a karlekammerskab linen closet painted sage green. Anchored to light, natural materials—hemp baskets, wood, cotton—the room feels spacious despite being generously stocked with colorful toys, masks, and tools for dress-up. Meanwhile, ceiling-mounted gymnastics rings by the Finnish brand Lillagunga bring the outdoor playground inside. ●

No More, No Less

Nothing more nor less than "the sum of its details." The Danish brand Oliver Furniture shows off the unparalleled beauty of things made by nature and by the human hand. The Scandinavian woodworking tradition is visible in pieces both classically crafted and thoroughly modern: Oliver clothes rails disappear behind larger garments that can't fit comfortably in a wardrobe. The brand's white-lacquered wardrobes are Nordic through and through, with rounded corners, invisible screws, integrated hooks, and flexible shelving, so universal that they fit anywhere. ●

PERLUDI

Max in the Box

Austrian furniture-maker Perludi transforms ordinary activities into play. Its indestructible, multitasking furniture is a cross between Donald Judd and Lincoln Logs in birch plywood, primary colors, loden wool textiles, and crisp geometric lines. The single bed Otto in the Moon becomes a bench when flipped over. Pauli is a modular seating, storage, and play station. Max in the Box, developed with kids, is a growing chair and table set, make-believe grocery store, bookshelf, or bedside table. Fold the low bunk bed, Amber in the Sky, if you like: its upholstery joins plywood components without glue or dowels. ●

Bunk Bed,
Not a Bunker

Oliver Furniture designed this
Scandinavian oak bed, in four
models, can be transformed into
a single bed. Aided by an elevated
ladder between beds and minimalist
railings that keep little ones safe
without looking armored, it also
makes what might have been a
heavy addition to the room feel light
and barely there. The design puts
pretty bedding patterns front and
center instead of a bulky monolith. ●

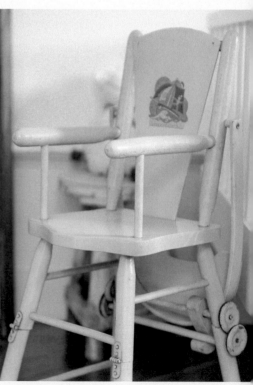

Beautifully Bare

If you want your child to live in spaces as natural and healthy as the clean food you feed them, take a look at IKEA's Flisat collection. Designed for three- to twelve-year-olds, the furniture is formally simple and materially rich. Barely finished pine retains all the beauty of its wood grain and features bright, saturated bits of color in the form of wall hooks or storage boxes. The pieces are customizable and multipurpose: the desk is available in three heights, while the dollhouse can be hung on the wall to be used as shelving when your little one grows out of it. ●

Play Areas

On the Bunk Bed, on the Carpet— Everywhere!

▲ Children are keen homebuilders: this framework from Müller Möbelwerkstätten is an ideal place to retreat and, with a cover, becomes a play den.

◀ Every child loves rocking—rocking animals come in a wide range of shapes and colors. This moose from IKEA makes the little one into a Sweden fan.

◀◀ Sleeping, working, or boxing all take place here on only a few square meters, with a padded windowsill for relaxing.

Living in a small space is normal for children. During childhood, activities that are later distributed over several spaces (sleeping, eating, working, and relaxing) take place—(hopefully) apart from eating—in the children's room. To facilitate all these activities in a single room, we advise parents to come up with a well-considered division of space that assigns a place for each activity. It is, of course, natural for such classifications to blur in day-to-day life. They do, however, ▶

Childhood activities need designated areas.

▼ help to achieve some form of basic order, which benefits both you and your child.

The fixed furnishings include a bed, table, and chair, along with space for storing clothing and playthings. It is nice when the firehouse has a regular place on a shelf, the stuffed animals always spend the night in a decorative basket, and books stand upright in crates or on a bookshelf. But it is even nicer when your child plays with them! And for that, space is necessary. We are not saying that every child has to have a big room—this is, incidentally, not the case for any of our own children. We are only saying that childhood activities need designated areas, even if they are still quite manageable.

Does your child like reading? Congratulations! A small sofa, an inviting chair, or even only a pile of cushions near the bookshelf is then just the thing for budding members of the educated classes. You can stage this area as a magical place with a sufficiently bright (but not glaring!) lamp. If there is no space for such an area, a reading corner can be set up directly on the bed. In this case, we recommend stowing ▶

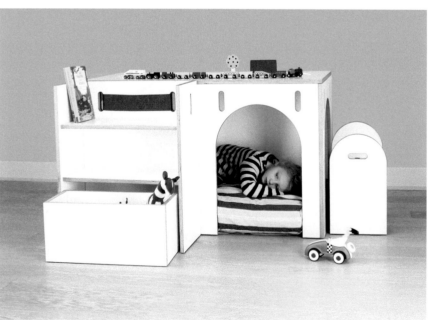

◀ Children's life in XS-format: the Archipel bed from jundado is a place to sleep, a cave, play surface, and storage space all rolled into one. The elements can be connected with one another in various ways by means of straps that are guided through the grip holes and fixed with Velcro fasteners.

Bottom: This desk of birch plywood with a top unit from Torafu Architects goes along with every mood and is one time a stage, another a dollhouse, and—when the serious side of life begins—a perfect place to do homework.

▲ Children's life in XL-format: every activity has its own generous place here. The berth-look components, the hammock, and the big pillow on the floor bring the comfort needed to this airy room.

▼ the blankets and pillows away during the day so that your child still has a feeling of going to bed in the evening, even if he or she has already spent a lot of time on the bed in the daytime.

And if your child is a master builder, give him or her enough free surfaces for setting up a colorful fantasy world unhindered. Whether such a free surface is a spacious center of the room or a compact shelf for giving life to a zoo or dollhouse is secondary to the fun that can be had.

Parents who would like to design things in a somewhat more refined way can get inspiration from a circus tent: a trapeze in the door lintel, rings at the center of the room, or wall bars (vintage pieces of ▶

◀ Everything refined: with a wealth of pillows, the child's bed becomes a reading nest during the day, the round carpet invites sprawling, and the shelf compartments at child-height are clearly structured and easy to reach.

▶ The dollhouse by Torafu Architects is a true all-rounder: when opened up, it is a small world for dolls and other figurines, and, when folded closed, provides storage space and serves as a chair.

◀ For very active children: at least two square meters of a children's room should be planned for a bouldering wall—great fun for young (and old).

▶ Climbing and sliding are absolute fun classics on the playground—how much better when there is also space for them in a children's room.

wood are especially beautiful) shorten any rainy afternoon for children who are hungry for movement. The particular advantage of such devices is that they only take up limited space.

And if there is no shortage of space, it is worth entering the search terms "bunk bed" and "slide" on Pinterest. There, you will find everything from the, admittedly, pretty-ugly to the phenomenal-fanciful. No matter what variant your child chooses: the hours that he or she spends climbing, jumping, and sliding in his or her room—whether alone, with friends, or with siblings—will not be forgotten. In the end, the same was true for us. ●

▲ The birch plywood ZooKids series from JULICA offers space for lots of friends. There is extra storage space in the stools, the table is simultaneously a cave, and it can also serve as a space to withdraw in rooms for adults.

◀ The classic among play zones is the space under a loft bed. Here, the area is kept tidy with a chest of drawers and baskets. The self-made tree adds a scouting flair.

▶ Felt stones are not only wonderful settings for many an adventure, but also great to sit on.

Under Construction

Max, Leon, and Tristan share a bedroom that encourages play and making. Playoffice tailored the space to the boys' favorite activities, while encouraging flights of fancy, accommodating each personality in different parts of the room. A table stocked with tools and craft materials forms a workshop area, while a bright yellow construction crane serves as the bed beside a tripartite loft space for play, including a reading loft, LEGO corner, and, below the crane, a closet for dress-up costumes. Embedded in the wall at floor level, a night-light is the house of "Perez Mouse." ●

PAMELA POMPLITZ

Staycation

In her son's gender-neutral nursery, stylist Pamela Pomplitz turned her old office into a crisp alpine scene, using a photographic mural—and an actual birch tree that "grows" in front of it. Mountain Morning by Uppsala Fototapet fills a corner, and the interior of an intimate sleeping nook, of this rustic-modern, snow-white bedroom, complete with a model cable car. Pomplitz echoes the sapphire sky on cushions, upholstery, a cabinet, and a pennant—using the mural to connect the cozy interior to an expansive exterior. ●

NIKOLINE DYRUP CARLSEN
& SVEND JACOB PEDERSEN

Making (Play) Space

To maximize play space, try maximizing storage. In Copenhagen, the TV show hosts and designers Nikoline Dyrup Carlsen and Svend Jacob Pedersen created a flexible layout that generates multiuse "activity zones" where every detail is both practical and whimsical. The hall is a fold-out cabinet, beds close into walls, desktops disappear when not in use, and the children's room doubles as a playground with a climbing wall and slide. A festive red-and-white, built-in cabinet hides closets, beds, toy storage, and play nooks. ●

Hideaway House

"We made it up as we went along," says Suzanne Harmar, who created this bunk-bed dwelling for her kids Sammuel and Dixie. Inspired by images on Pinterest, Instagram, and design blogs, she first mapped the plan of their hideaway on the floor using masking tape. Then she cut it out of an MDF sheet and placed it over a structure of IKEA bed slats. The stairs were another IKEA hack, from kitchen cupboards with an LED strip for a night-light. White passivating paint neutralized the chemicals in the MDF, and color was added via wall hooks, Farg Form bedding, Normann Copenhagen wall pockets, and cozy cushions. ●

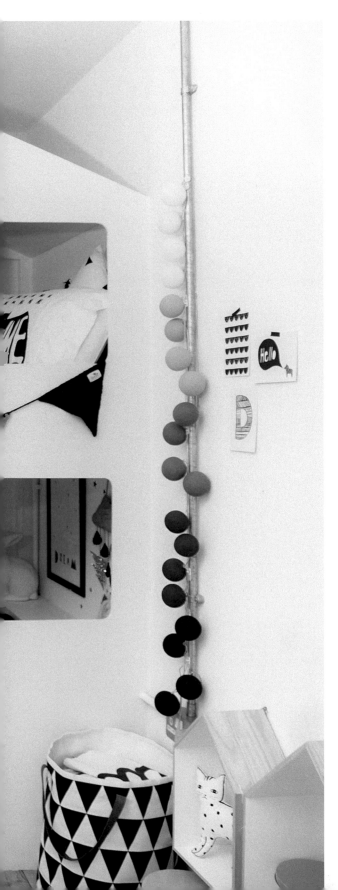

137

Little Worka- holics

Artworks, Homework, Learning Concentration

L aptop, framed photos, a pencil case, newspapers, the obligatory coffee cup, and other fetishized objects: charismatic adult desks often attract attention due to a concentration of objects and the fact that the multiple, parallel activities of its owner are spread out almost like a tableau.

For children, who are totally overtaxed by multitasking but still do many different things on their tables, it is important, in contrast, to create a workspace that is initially as empty as ▶

▲ Beautiful at home as well: there is now an extensive stock of vintage school furniture. A lot of it has additional storage space for notebooks and pencils under the desktop.

▶ Make use of space! Not only in the city, where living space is becoming ever scarcer, it makes sense to repurpose space under a sloping roof or niches as a workspace with only a few resources.

▶▶ A folding table that can be mounted on the wall with hinges takes up barely any space. The same applies in the case of the picture gallery made from simple wire: pictures can dry here and regularly be replaced with new ones. Children love hanging up their works!

▲ This old school desk has space for two children. Make sure to always have enough bins nearby so that children can tidy up themselves again once they have finished working.

▶ The turquoise desk goes perfectly with the pink color of the wall. A bulletin board above the desk provides space for drawings and messages from friends.

▼ possible, where they learn to concentrate on one thing. When they master this eventually, they are inevitably better equipped for the demands of school and working life.

The table should therefore have a basically empty surface and compartments nearby or directly on the desk where pens, paper, and other work materials can be stored for easy access. There are numerous tables for children on the market—from economically priced but very pretty IKEA models, to vintage pieces, to the adjustable desk classic by Egon Eiermann (available from Richard Lampert). The latter features a practical cart with wheels and an orthopedically tested and adjustable chair as well.

When choosing a chair, it is important to ensure that the child is able to place feet flat on the floor and elbows on the desktop so that the upper and lower arms approximately form a right angle when sitting with a straight back.

Besides adequate lighting (from the left for right-handers, and from the right for left-handers), the question of location is decisive. We always encourage parents to make use of existing niches or uninspiring locations over a radiator and under a window, turning them into a working surface by means of simple installations (all that is actually necessary is a securely mounted board). Since children enjoy joint activities as well, it is also ideal to have siblings or friends sitting next to one another comfortably—the only thing required is simply a somewhat longer board.

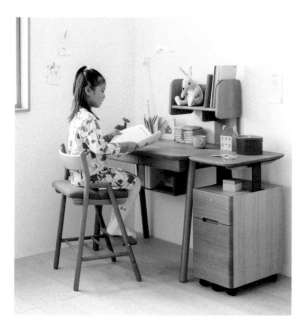

▲ The play station: such a big table is wonderful for doing arts and crafts, writing, or eating together. With such a table, people who have sufficient space can guarantee hours of creative activity.

◀ Ideal for the start of school: this Cobrina desk from Torafu Architects was created in cooperation with Hida Sangyo, a Japanese furniture maker. The storage system helps keep things organized. Many of the compartments can be assembled individually, something that children enjoy.

For limited space, we recommend a folding desk (such as by Müller Möbelwerkstätten). Desks of this kind may also be situated in a room for adults, like in the living room, and be easily folded down again when work is done. The good thing about this solution is that parents can keep an eye on children when they are doing homework, for example. Since children just love to sit on the floor, they will surely occasionally end up there in spite of having a nice desk corner. As always, a ▶

▲ A wall sculpture of one's favorite animal: this model from Lago has numerous storage compartments as well as a work surface. It is also possible to position a lamp in an ideal way, with the light optimally coming from the left for right-handers and vice versa.

◀ Vintage wonderland—parents particularly love nostalgic wooden toys. On this table, a small child can engage in creative activities for a few hours.

▶ The modern variant is just as practical: pencils and such can also quickly vanish under the work surface.

▼ couple of basic rules for children's rooms also help in this case. Homework and messy activities like kneading clay or painting with watercolors should definitely be done on a table. Simple arts and crafts or board games can also take place on the floor. As comfortable as being on the floor might seem to children—stooping over damages the still-growing spine in the long run. Nor is working on the floor good for the eyes, since the lighting situation is rarely optimal. Also, children often cast shadows themselves. Whether on the floor or a table: the most important thing is to teach them to stow their materials away again in the designated place once the activity is finished. ●

▶ This one-legged table is an ideal solution for corners, can be mounted on the wall, and is also big enough for two children.

▼ The space under the window and over a radiator is used in an optimal way by means of a carpentered, custom-made solution and is now equipped with compartments, a work surface, and storage space. The desk also makes it possible to work in small groups.

◀ Industrial-style vintage furniture: this narrow table here becomes more of a chic console either for displaying treasures or for working after tidying up.

Bottom left: Cover closed—the table from the Müller Möbelwerkstätten has an integrated light and work compartments. The height of the chair can be adjusted and grows along with the child. This gives it particular orthopedic value.

▶ A hallway solution: when staged so beautifully, a small children's table, such as this model from Ferm Living, also does not get in the way in a transit zone. Children who quickly get distracted in their own room by the playthings there are often able to concentrate better on homework outside their rooms.

▼ This custom-made table variant fulfills several requirements at the same time. It delimits the space toward the sofa, holds firewood, and provides space for offspring and their first writing exercises.

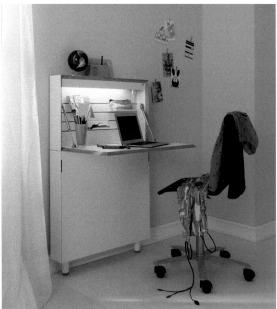

PURE POSITION

Stages of Growth

Like the growing bed, Pure Position's three-piece growing table works on the principle that a baby's environment should grow up with the baby. The legs of the table, stool, and bench can be adjusted to four heights via a simple screw system. A handsome, blond table that is 24 mm thick—made of birch plywood and abrasion-resistant coating—features movable containers for pens, books, and other objects. A reel on the left side of the table allows for the insertion of a roll of paper that can be spread flat across the table for easy art-making, whether it is one child working solo or two jointly. ●

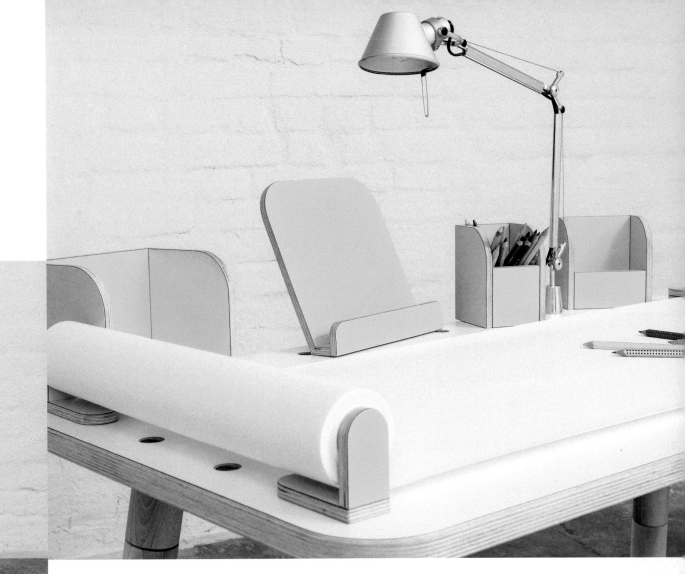

147

OLIVER FURNITURE

The Grasshopper

Live slower. Oliver Furniture creates products "rooted in carefree summer days, high blue skies, waves splashing on the shore, echoes in the cool green forest, and the comfort of time spent with friends and family." With clean lines, soft but sturdy shapes, and delicate yet practical details, it makes a virtue of simplicity. The junior office table offers generous storage, and when the kids' legs grow, its legs can, too. The bench has a bellyful of storage hidden in the seat—and, though great for the children' room, it also works in the entryway or living room and plays well with almost any other product, Oliver or not. ●

Love for Lola

Lola's room was a labor of love.
After tearing up the floor, designers
Holly Marder and Hedda Pier of
Avenue Design Studio painted the
room white and Farrow & Ball's Light
Blue to make it bright and airy,
but calming, too. They sanded the
second-hand bed and used a roller
and sponge to cover it in radiator
paint. Color is found in personal and
vintage objects: a red crinoline hung
in a frame like a painting, a shaggy
carpet's colorful triangles echoed
in a beaded African basket on Lola's
space-saving shelf-desk, a string
with clothespins as a display for her
finger paintings, and, not least,
a garland of pom-poms. ●

JUSTINE GLANFIELD

Scavenger Hunt

Justine Glanfield, a veteran furniture scavenger and designer of Lacoste knitwear and Cotton & Milk, has filled her son Oscar's double-height room in Brussels with a tidy mishmash of flea market treasures. Her finds include a toy car park and puppet theater from the 1950s. Glanfield is resourceful: Oscar's hip clothes, hung on the walls, double-task as design accents, a disused fireplace serves as a bookshelf, bed cushions are sewn from curtain fabric, and a linen tablecloth is transformed into a curtain. ●

153

Midcentury Multifunctional

The Japanese studio Torafu adds clever structure to kids' design. Kol is a dollhouse or bookshelf when open, and a chair when closed. The Koloro desk resembles a dollhouse, birdhouse, or Guignol stage but is a portable, highly personalizable workspace with magnetic windows in its walls to modulate privacy. The Cobrina desk collection has a rounded softness that camouflages lots of storage, while Dice is a desk that becomes a stool for grown-ups when a panel is extended, or a bookshelf when rotated. Panel edges and faces are painted different colors, so each function gives Dice a new look. ●

Masterfully Simple

Victoire's bedroom is almost completely white. This bright retreat, created by the owner of the online shop Yellow Flamingo for his daughter, is offset by a creamy rose coverlet and fabric storage bin. A subdued seaglass-green dado anchors her work desk. The designer opted for an unusual wall lamp: a knitted ropy fixture by Llot Llov called Matt that Victoire hangs from a strap mounted to the wall beside the bed. Moreno eliminated clutter, using only two simple, small shelves and providing the room with an empty spaciousness that invites play, rest, reflection, and imagination. ●

Sustainable Design

Want to give your little person a hand in choosing the spaces and furniture they spend time in and with? Afilii stocks a cherry-picked universe of kids' furniture in natural materials by international designers and labels—Casie Living, de Breuyn, Fnurst—whose pieces are minimal but highly adaptable, designed to promote creativity, independence, and motor-skill development: the sustainable, growing Lumy bed by Ekomia, Coclico's line based on the Montessori learning method, handcrafted furniture by PRINZENKINDER, or the modular Archipel series, a multifunctional play island, by Jundado. ●

Pure Detail

From 2012, the Danish furniture label OYOY has been honoring diverse inspirations: Scandinavian clarity, Japan's sophisticated simplicity, Native American Hopi geometries, childhood memories, journeys, and landscapes. Animals flourish on placemats, mobiles, and among vivid palettes, pared-down patterns, and pure materials like organic cotton. A clever trick: the lion poster is actually a framed tea towel! Bedding includes stuffed giraffes, fabric mobiles, and cushions. ●

OYOY

Pattern Play

From soothing linens to exciting essentials, ferm LIVING's Kids accessories bespeak whimsy near and far. The collections range from an energizing terrazzo-print lunchbox, pencil case, and gym bag to exotic Fruiticana wallpaper, knitted cushions, rattles, and music mobiles in organic cotton and metallic finishes. They also feature baskets, nursing pillows, and GOTS-certified cotton bed linens. Wallpaper hangs easily with ready-made paste, and decorative wood-frame foldaway tents ensure playtime privacy with window blinds. ●

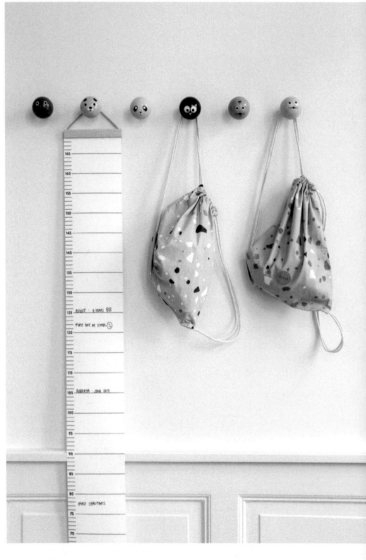

Nightlife

Falling Asleep, Sleeping through the Night, Co-Sleeping

Sleep is a major issue in childhood: finding a sleeping rhythm, learning to sleep alone, overcoming fear of the dark. Many families practice rituals for falling asleep: songs are sung, or stories read—and, naturally, there is then cuddling before bidding farewell for the night.

Nevertheless, years often elapse before children fall asleep in their own bed, in their own room, and also actually sleep through the night there. This process of letting go is generally interrupted by phases in their parents' bed—whether during the breastfeeding period or, later, because of nightmares or various aches and pains. Some families even intentionally practice co-sleeping, where parents and children sleep together in one big family bed or on different beds spread out in one room—like farming families in the Middle Ages. We do not want to promote any particular sleeping model here: as long as all members of a family get enough sleep, and are thus even-tempered during the day, anything is permissible.

So that children feel at ease in their own beds, it is important to create a cozy atmosphere. This can be achieved by means of simple ingredients such as ▶

◀ Rolling dreams: this wooden bed from Perludi is easy to move from one room to the next. The soft outer walls of felt are child-friendly.

▶ The uuio VII bed; modern, sleek and designed to grow with your child. The exchangeable frame parts allow you to adjust it to your child's height.

◀◀ Climbing, jumping, sleeping: the R&R bed combo from Rafa-kids, consisting of one raised and one single bed with wheels, encourages lots of activities and matches many interiors with its light wood.

◀ Rocking the baby in the crib, nursing, and singing lullabies often alternate with one another, which is why parents can do themselves a favor with an armchair nearby the crib.

▼ With this self-welded bed featuring a roof, children can hang all kinds of things on the poles— but above all delight in the idea of having a house of their own.

this generally takes place in a horizontal position.

Most children at some point want an adventurous place to sleep—suitable options are, naturally, meanwhile available from various producers: a tree-house bed (for instance by Mathy by Bols), a car bed (by Vipack), or a hanging tent (by Haba). Parents who shy away from such an investment can find a different solution: with a curtain, a normal single bed can be retrofitted as a canopy bed, while a large pirate flag turns a bed into a pirate ship. ▶

▼ soft textiles (beautiful bed linens, for example by Georg Jensen Damask), pleasant colors, and positioning the head end of the bed against one wall of the room. After the crib, we recommend simple beds that grow along with the child— hence a cot that becomes a child's bed at some point (for instance from Laurette or IKEA).

Later on—if the size of the room allows—we encourage parents to directly purchase a bed in adult size. First of all, children find such beds wonderful; second, a small overnight guest can also sleep in it; and third, a child's room may, when necessary, be repurposed as a guest room—in large-city apartments, where families often live in limited space, this is a very practical solution when no separate guest room is available. Moreover, a big bed is important particularly for teenagers, since eating, playing on the cell phone, doing homework—all of

▼Young overnight guests love it when they encounter a sleeping scenario based on the twin principle. That means: two sets of the same bed linens, a stuffed animal on the pillow for each child, and, if the space permits, two small night tables with a lamp and a water glass. With a few easy steps, it is thus possible to give a visiting child the feeling that he or she is welcome, and to help the child in the case of possible homesickness. ●

▲ Soft colours and 100% cotton blankets by Rose in April brings a dream-like poetry to sleeping spaces.

Most children want an adventurous place to sleep.

◀ This wooden cradle is a rocking piece of carpentry for very young children.

▲ The main thing is that it's out of the ordinary: a comfortable niche for dreaming has here been constructed under a sloping roof. The area beneath provides lots of storage space for playthings.

Top left: Whether for stuffed animals or overnight guests—these beds fit into any corner.

▲ This two-story house bed is self-built and provides all kinds of space for playing, climbing, and hiding. The space under the steps is perfect for stowing things away.

◀ In this cool trailer, there are storage shelves, a door that can be closed, and even a sliding roof. The only thing that's still missing is a campsite and a starry sky.

▶ Co-sleeping, head to head: being able to hear the breathing of others is a good feeling and makes this a good solution for consecutive siblings.

▼ UFO with screen: this UFO, on which it is possible to play and which has a bed with its own TV underneath, is a nocturnal landscape that definitely also pleases older children.

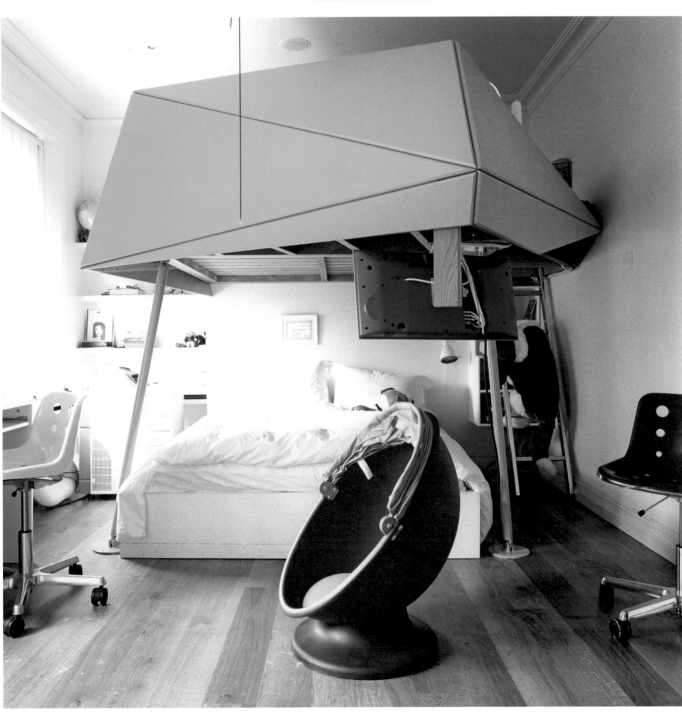

179

▲ A nostalgic children's room: girls in particular love canopies, curtains, and tents. Here is a felicitous mixture of patterns and fabrics that emanates coziness with its dark colors.

▶ A sumptuously draped canopy, decorative rabbit lamps, and night tables on the right and left: this luxury variant of sleeping for children achieves the cozy formality of a hotel.

◀ Airy white also works in children's rooms. This single bed in a niche in front of the window also leaves space for other furnishings such as a towel rack and a chair.

Playwood

At only 17 square meters, Matteo's little room is big in efficiency and full of opportunities for discovery and play. Jäll & Tofta used the full height of the room to build a house within a house, including a bunk bed and a desk that runs the full length of the room. The built-in furniture is equipped with hidden storage space in the staircase and desk, so that taking toys out and putting them away again feels like burying or hunting for treasure. Made from graphically grainy maritime plywood against a whitewashed timber floor and walls, the space is built for one or two children. ●

JÄLL & TOFTA

Room for Roommates

Caspar shares this bedroom with his younger sister. To fill the space efficiently, the German studio Jäll & Tofta created a white, oiled pinewood loft bed against a marigold wall. It contains sleeping areas for both kids, along with storage—but all in a space that feels like a bright, magical cave. A staircase cum toy cabinet accesses the top bunk while a circular opening accesses the bottom, with another smaller, circular cutout offering a secret view out the side. Across from the window, a bespoke pine shelf makes space for books and a nook for reading and chilling out. ●

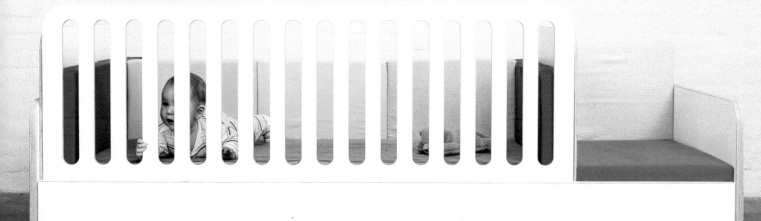

Stages of Life

Become a cushion architect. Pure Position's growing bed ages with your child, adapting through the day's activities and through the seasons of maturing. Then, when the little one has grown big, it can retire into use as a sofa for the whole family. Its modularity and stability make it—with three mattresses and smart upholstery system—eminently versatile as a sofa with a nest-like enclosure for a baby, a playpen, a guest bed, or all of the above. The result is a self-contained environment that is secure and sustainably produced, embracing the family in color and softness. ●

Make it Mellow

▼ Pastel colours bring softness to sleeping spaces that encourages children to melt comfortably into nap times. Washes of pinks and yellows punctuated with colour make for a poetic dream-like environment whilst wild scatterings of illustrateed, sleeping pillows turn the linen into slumbering companions. The varnished pine shelves hung with black metal wire designed by Rose in April add a retro and elegant finish to a cosy nap space.

Where the Wild Things Are

▼ Go where the wild things are. Populate the room with lighthearted illustrations and the plush forms of Scandinavian forest animals like Mr. Moose. Pared-down and pastel, Nordic Bloomingville Mini or Kids textiles, toys, tableware, cushions, and accessories are conceived for design-oriented youngsters and tweens.

Adventure awaits!

JÄLL & TOFTA

Smart Storage

Cleanliness is next to cabinetry. Isn't that how the saying goes? To keep Jasper's room tidy, the designer included lots of storage, even storing away the guest bed in an alcove and storing the reading area in a cosy niche, too. To suit the open, high-ceilinged space, the designer scaled up the bespoke desk and bed and also created corners to provide moments of shelter. This cosiness is heightened via fields of green paint that define zones wrapping the bed and alcoves, as well as through the use of organic materials like wood, wool, and linen. ●

Ply Playroom

Plyroom's kids' furnishings share blond, natural birch surfaces, a sleek carpenterly look with joinery elements, and a lightweight solidity—handsome, secure, and often convertible. The Ava Lifestages cot—eco-friendly, forestry-certified, and non-toxic—can adapt from an adjustable two-height crib into a junior bed and modern desk, without extra parts or headaches. The Sleigh single bed is a crib that grows into a bed, which slides comfortably between the legs of the Dream Cloud loft bed. During game time, the Australian-made Peggy Pegboard is a play surface that endlessly fires the imagination. ●

Down the Rabbit Hole

Functional furniture and decorating accessories and textiles are the fruits of a collaboration between the French magazine Milk and the furniture brand Habitat. The furnishings (including a bunk with trundle bed and a tent) and accessories (from cushions and linens to lidded boxes and partly painted baskets) combine natural oak with a subdued palette that pairs cornflower blue and mustard. The graphical patterns riff on bunnies, even in the form of bedside lamps, while the outlines of gabled houses become shelves and nightstands. ●

Clever Accents

▲ Accented with doses of happy color throughout, this white Berlin bedroom features a blue rug with racetrack pattern, a flag garland, and the Eames' Hang It All wall hooks in poppy shades next to his Elephant Stool (both produced by Vitra). Colors pop out of otherwise blank surfaces, complimented, through large windows, by the emerald hues of the garden. Two mushroom-patterned dollhouses serve as whimsical storage boxes, while the bunk bed is shaped like a timber-sided house. Another source of cheer? Unobtrusive shelves on which books are stored with their covers facing into the room instead of their spines.

Made to Measure

Like an invisible friend that can grow up too, Ekomia's Lumy growing bed is made of FSC-certified solid pinewood from Sweden, washable organic cotton and sheep's wool, natural latex, coconut, and dyes. Its height (and firmness) are adjustable and two wheels make it portable. All-white or white with candy colors, the slatted frame comes raised. After three years, it can be lowered and converted to keep the little one from falling out. At five years, a kit—with a Phillips screwdriver, hammer, 13 mm wrench, or pliers—turns it into a junior bed. From there, it may make a good daybed. ●

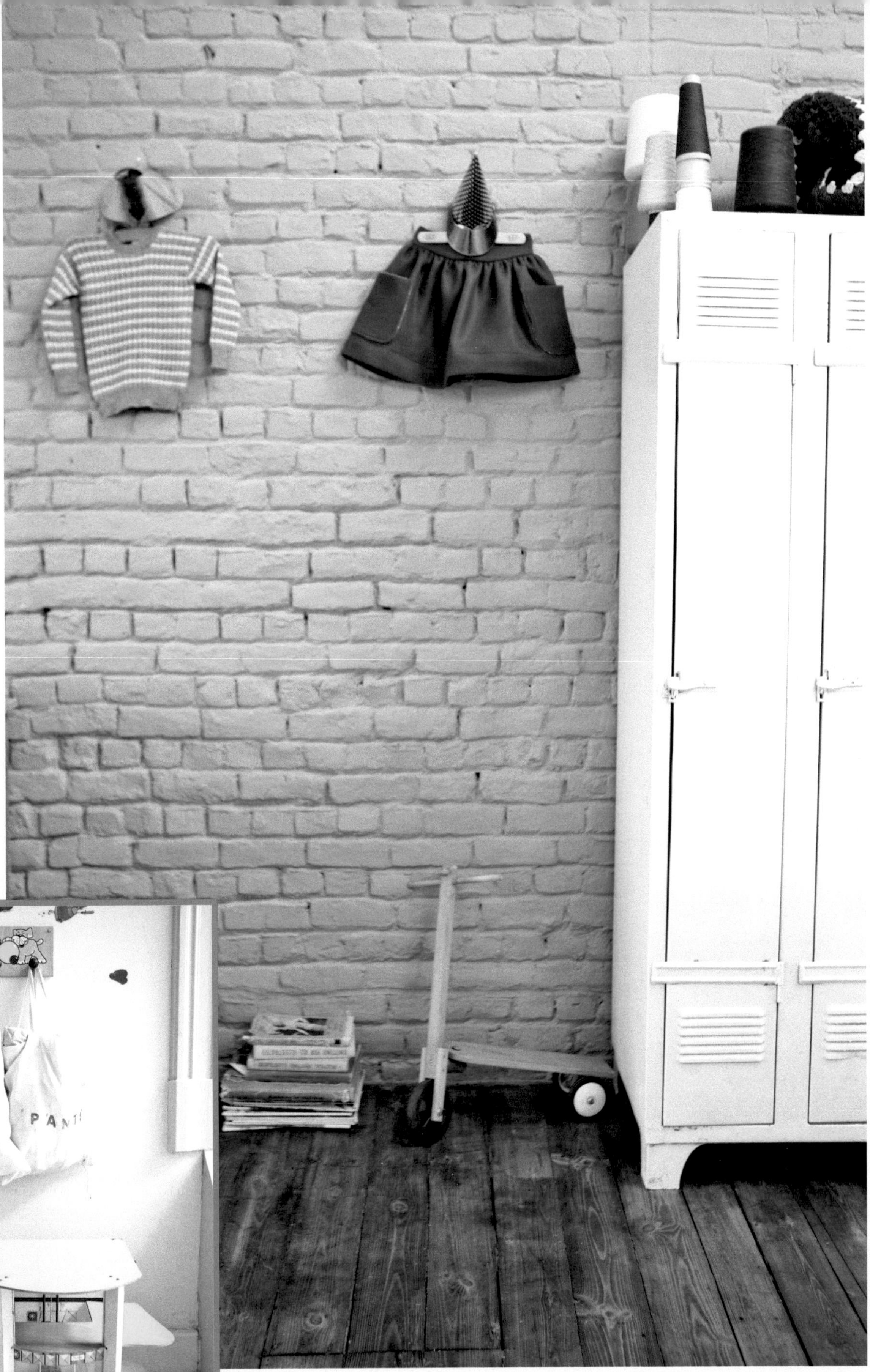

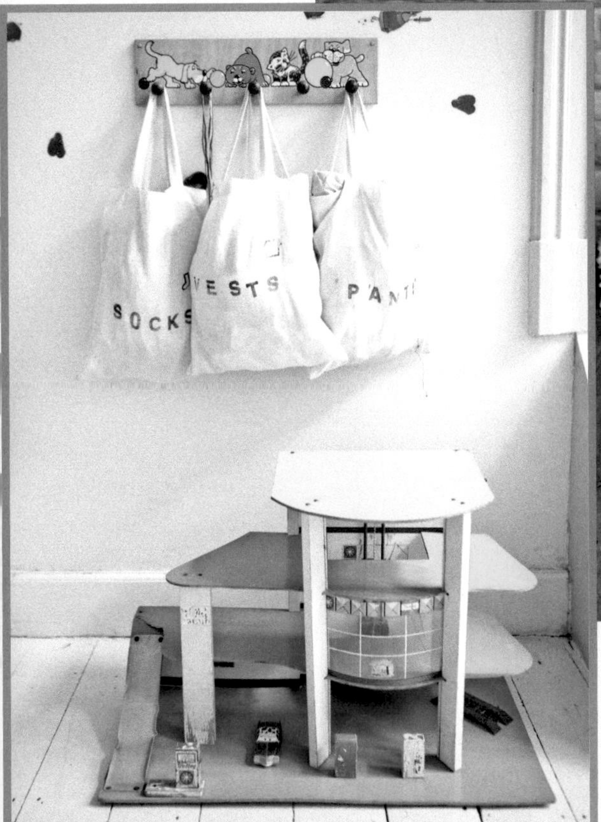
SOCKS
VESTS

SEBRA

For the Modern Romanticist

The classic Juno bed, designed in the early 1940s by Danish architect Viggo Einfeldt, has grown up. Which is exactly what Einfeldt designed it to do in the first place. Ranked among 108 iconic Danish designs for kids, the bed has now been updated with modern functionality. The Sebra is larger and features a height-adjustable bottom that can grow from baby to toddler and junior. It is safer, too: while meeting the European safety standard DS/EN 716, it is also coated with an antibacterial, eco-friendly wood paint. This means a healthier indoor environment for everyone. ●

BABETTE LEERTOUWER

Restorative Design

Using simple details and lovingly renewing old objects, the designer and stylist Babette Leertouwer transformed a plain room in Baarn, Netherlands, into a rustic-modern nursery. She wrote the little boy's name, Luca, in rope above his wooden-ship-shaped cradle and restored the dresser with a new coat of paint and rope handles. Wall-mounted simple wooden boxes serve as shelves that also frame the pretty objects situated there, like a colorful abacus. Leertouwer also drew an airplane and a hot-air balloon on the computer to make wall stickers. ●

211

A Careful Edit

Delight is in the details! In a bright
white and pale cornflower blue room,
multiple playlands are united to
a single coherent interior: the
schoolroom with world map, antique
wooden desk and chalkboard, and
a tepee complete with knot cushions
and a feathered headdress. Wall text
is written in cursive neon. A three-
tiered shelf holds knit dolls, a set of
matryoshka dolls, and a wooden car
with movable wheels. On the
mantelpiece, a set of wooden blocks
is hand-painted with alphabet
letters or images: a bumblebee,
a strawberry, a silk top hat. ●

Room for a Cosmopolitan Rustic

Eclectic and urbane aren't often used to describe baby products, but they fit the contents of San Francisco's Aldea home and baby decor shop. This rustic-contemporary vignette from the 2013 catalog, meant to inspire clients and even DIY ideas, includes the Oeuf Sparrow crib and midcentury-inspired Mini Storage Library, along with a matching dresser and changing table. The stylists tuck in clever tips, leaving the walls roughly textured, crafting display shelves by standing a canoe on end, and injecting color via a world-map area rug. ●

YOU
MAKE
ME
HAPPY
WHEN
SKIES
ARE GRAY

EMILIE MUNROE

Animal Kingdom

A tall floor lamp resembles nothing so much as a giraffe, overlooking the dark-wood crib of this nursery. Dark wood surfaces are combined with white paint and a carpet singing with bold stripes of color. The bed linens are illustrated with a menagerie of comforting creatures, along with an elephant cushion, and hippo, lion, and Moomintroll-like toys crafted in leather. A metal trunk in Curious George-yellow provides storage and seating. ●

For Baby and Me

In this bedroom, the designer created a synthesis of the grown-up and the child-like: lemon yellow blob paintings in sleek black frames hang next to a midcentury brass starburst chandelier. Beside a lathe-turned side table, a classic contemporary armchair in charcoal upholstery is echoed by a small-scale version with a pink seat. Baby's senses are stimulated by a sheep mobile, a yellow tabletop elephant bookshelf, a seahorse lamp, a red-and-white stuffed fish afloat in the wooden crib, and a circular area rug, radiating multiple subdued colors. ●

Race-y Room

In Kentfield, California, Benjamin snuggles into a scarlet race car when he goes to sleep each night. To give the room "a race-day feel," Emilie Munroe printed a stock photo of an F1 race car that she found on Shutterstock. Then she installed the custom mural at an angle across one wall, arranging the bed to look as if it were driving into the room. Other playful details include a pom-pom fringed giraffe lamp, Mason nightstands from Room&Board, big metal letters and yellow shelving from The Land of Nod, Vioski's Palms I Chair, the Devon six-drawer dresser from Newport Cottages, and a beanbag by Leong Interiors. ●

Building Character

Studio Munroe modernized this
San Francisco residence while
respecting the historical
architecture of the building.
The son's room glows with
corals, sky blue, sun-kissed
orange, and kelly and mint
greens, as well as a mix
of patterns and textures.
The designers decorated with
the Woven Owl Hamper and
the Half Shell Turtle Floor Bin
by The Land of Nod, a carved-
wood side table from West Elm,
and the Lattice Flokati Rug
from Anthropologie. They also
added flat Roman shades
from The Shade Store, a
Daredevil Ovo table lamp from
Lamps Plus, and the Versus
galvanized trunk from CB2. ●

ALDEA HOME + BABY

King of My Castle

You'll never guess who lives in this bedroom! Andiamo is a Peruvian-made, Vespa-owning, spaghetti-eating Italian (knit) dog. His (and his little girl's) room is anchored by a compact Perch bunk bed by Oeuf from Aldea Baby that recedes under the room's decor—garlands of felt flags, patterned cushions, children's paintings—and numerous other plush inhabitants. The five-star amenity is an eco-friendly Bamboo Sunshine dollhouse by Hape. Its modernist architecture includes three portable Lucite room separators and a functional solar panel that powers LED lights inside the house. ●

Young at Heart

LAGO's mantra: "Never stop becoming kids." The Italian brand uses solids and voids to make sustainable furniture, from magically cantilevering minimalist beds to graphical shelving, desks that are just an outline defining a space of imagination, and wardrobes that consist of patchworks of color. Beds like Gizmo, Fluttua, and Cloud float in a corner, perch atop a single height-adjustable leg, and drift along in a perfect sky. The Linea bed comes in a treehouse version that opens up floor and wall space around it. ●

LAGO

Technē Architecture + Interior Design

 With humor and elegance, Technē architects added a nursery to this Art Deco house in Melbourne. They opted for a dark forest-green carpet, a Togo armchair by Ligne Roset, a modernist wooden crib with transparent sides for easy baby monitoring, and a stool in the shape of a partly eaten cob of corn.

Ham Interiors Team

▼ The pastel interiors of a Devon fisherman's cottage compliment the mercurial iridescence of the seashore. Ham Interiors colored this children's room like a freshly cut watermelon, mixing celadon and minty green blinds with a rose area rug and walls in blushing white tones with red-striped cushions.

Stylish & Cozy

▶ The uuio VII bed; modern, sleek and designed to grow with your child. The exchangeable frame parts allow you to adjust it to your child's height.

JOANNA BAGGE

Making space

It's far from hyperbole: this intelligent interior is hyper-efficient, hyper-handsome, and hyper-comfortable. In stylist Joanna Bagge's two-room, 68-square-meter apartment in Gothenburg, Sweden, are beds, built-in storage, a smart partition, and storage solutions—so as to "make" space for a family of four (and accommodate all four in one bedroom). Using sleek black Valchromat, glass, and white-lacquered MDF (accented with colorful objects like a monkey lamp), he turned a once tight space into a bright, generous one. ●

OLIVER FURNITURE

Classical Contemporary

Set aside trends and ephemeral themes to meet real needs: Oliver Furniture has a classical familiarity and elegant contemporaneity. Using solid FSC-certified oak and birch or white-oiled Nordic oak, items like the Wood Mini+ bed let little people pretend they're sleeping in a big person's bed. With no effort, a bunk bed becomes two singles. A junior bed converts—chip, chop!—into a lounger. The Wood Mini+ low loft bed gives sleepers lots of space without overpowering the rest of the room. And when kids outgrow it, a simple conversion kit transforms it into a daybed or a small sofa. ●

238

Room to Grow

Like making pencil marks on the wall as they get taller, you may help your child feel like a grown-up by sleeping in a bed—IKEA's extendable Minnen—that can grow with them from the time they start to walk right into their tweens. But then, because they're actually still little, wrap them up in the durable, cool, soft, organic cotton percale Gran duvet and pillowcase set (which comes in its own beribboned fabric pouch), along with a GOTS-certified cotton muslin blanket from Sweden's Fine Little Day. ●

BAILEY MCCARTHY

Set the Stage

Designer Bailey McCarthy and stylist Rebecca Omweg scripted an emphatically scenographic interior for this bedroom shared by two kids. Hypergraphical blue patterns adorn the walls, trim moldings, and outline bunk beds. The bespoke carpet and an armchair-ottoman set are shades of blue, too. Cole & Son's Cambridge Stripe sheathes one wall crowned with a multicolored, carnivalesque blown-glass chandelier. Fabrics also play leading roles: Pierre Frey Arty Multicolore 01 curtain fabric for the Roman shades and clashingly scarlet Biscuit Home linens. ●

Playground of Patterns

Mustard and tourmaline paint soak this bedroom in jewel tones, while vivaciously patterned textiles (paisleys, Moghul-themed motifs) bring it to life. The walls are in a vivid sea green; the bedding, in ochre. Drapes enclosing the bunk beds—lined with fuschia paint and accessed by a pair of arches like a classical Renaissance tower—sport a ruby and sapphire floral pattern. Decor includes children's award ribbons, street signs ("Detour"), and a tailor's mannequin that has been turned into a floor lamp with the simple addition of a shade. ●

Storybook Bedding

▼ Decorator David Netto illustrated the playroom and kids' bedroom in this Los Angeles guest house a with storybook pattern and texture. The bedroom, just under the steep gable of the house, features four beds with alternating pink and blue quilts over a striped burgundy and purple carpet. One wall is tattooed with amorphous globs of color, matching the curtains in the playroom (where they accompany Josef Frank upholstery). Fabulous furniture—Harry Bertoia's wire chair and diminutive brass floor lamps—completes the picture.

Bright Childhood

▼ In this luminous shared bedroom, Peek & Pack decorated with sunlight. The designers used existing windows to let it pour inside (hanging driftwood mobiles from their brass handles to float on the breeze) and painted the walls a radiant, blank-paper white. Masks of animal faces—a panda bear, a bear, a tiger—look out from the brick wall. Flanked with industrial-looking reading lights, the blond wood beds rest against a wallpaper depicting the world's architectural wonders as if they were hieroglyphs.

Space for the Imagination

▼ These Madrid children's rooms—playful but practical—steep growing minds in art and design. Sandonis used Origami lights by Studio Snowpuppe and whimsical wall-mounted masks among neutral surfaces, natural materials (wood, iron, and cotton), and dollhouse furnishings at human scale: an Oeuf NYC bed with gabled canopy, a handmade Iron House bed, and NOFRED wallpaper.

Index

ferm LIVING
fermliving.com

p. 86 top
pp. 166–171

HABITAT
habitat.com

p. 34 bottom
p. 49 top
pp. 196–199

hám interiors
haminteriors.com

p. 233

Marjon Hoogervorst
vorstin.nl

photography: Marjon Hoogervorst
p. 177 right

House of Pictures
houseofpictures.dk

production: Emma Persson
Lagerberg/House of Pictures
photography: Andrea Papini/House
of Pictures
p. 6
p. 9
pp. 18–19

Idea & styling: Louise Kamman
Riising/House of Pictures
Fotos: Pernille Kaalund/House of Pictures
spaconandx.com
p. 127 bottom
pp. 134–135

Inter IKEA Systems B.V.
ikea.com

pp. 118–121

The Interior Archive
interiorarchive.com

p. 12 photography: Nicolas Matheus/Cote
Paris, design: Laurence Dougier

pp. 24, 47 photography: Joanna
Maclennan, design: Fabienne Collombel

p. 25 photography: Edina van der Wyck,
architecture: Josh Schweitzer

pp. 35 bottom, 40–41 photography:
Alexander James, design: Oliver Burns

p. 44 top photography:
Jeltje Janmaat/House of Pictures,
design: Iris Rietbergen

pp. 46 top, 54–55 photography:
Luke White/The Irish at Home,
design: Ros Walshe

p. 122 photography: Frederic Vasseur/Cote
Paris, design: Catherine Schmidt

p. 125 photography: Fritz von der
Schulenburg, design: Philip Hooper

p. 138 bottom photography:
Jeltje Janmaat/House of Pictures

p. 177 top left photography:
Frederic Vasseur/Private Places/Jacqui
Small Collection, Design: David Berg

pp. 177 bottom left, 210–211
photography: Jeltje Janmaat/House of
Pictures, design: Babette Leertouwer

p. 178 bottom photography:
Alexander James

p. 179 bottom photography: Luke White,
design: Ab Rogers

p. 180 top photography:
Joanna Maclennan, Design, Miss Clara

p. 180 bottom photography: Luke White

Jäll & Tofta
jaellundtofta.de

photography:
Anne-Catherine Scoffoni
pp. 143
p. 183 top right and bottom
p. 192

photography: Anne Deppe
p. 182
p. 183 top left
p. 184
p. 185 top and bottom
p. 193

JULICA
JULICA-design.de

photography: Matthias Ritzmann
pp. 87
pp. 98–99
p. 129 top

LAGO
lago.it

Cover
pp. 142 top
pp. 226–231

Anna Landstedt
annalandstedt.com

interior design and photography:
Anna Landstedt
pp. 44 top
pp. 74–75
p. 86 bottom
pp. 104–107
p. 144

Jolene Lindner
jlidst.com

interior design: Jolene Lindner
photography: Thomas Kuoh
p. 140 bottom

Index

pure position,
a Label of IWL Machtlfing
pureposition.de

pp. 146–147
pp. 188–189

Rafa-kids
Rafa-kids.com

p. 174

Reiner Light Agency
reinerlight.com

photography: Victoria Pearson
p. 8

Rose in April
roseinapril.com

p. 176
p. 190

Sebra
sebra.dk

interior design: Sebra Interior
styling: styleplay.dk
photography: Anna Overholdt Hansen
p. 9 top
p. 123 bottom
pp. 206–209

Sian Zeng
sianzeng.com

p.45 top
p.48
pp. 66–69

Sigmar London
sigmarlondon.com

photography: Erica Bergsmeds
p. 23

Stil & Rum
stilorum.se

photography: Anders Bergstedt
pp. 240–241

Studio Revolution
studio-revolution.us

interior design: Studio Revolution
photography: Thomas Kuoh
pp. 26–27
p. 34 top
p. 129 bottom

Studio ROOF
studioroof.com

p. 4 bottom
p. 45 bottom

Espen Surnevik
espensurnevik.no

architecture:Espen Surnevik
photography: Ragnar Hartvig
p. 9 bottom
pp. 96–97
p. 144 bottom right

Polina Soloveichik
polinasoloveichik.com

painting: Polina Soloveichik
photography: Leon Kopplow
pp. 70–71

Techne Architecture
+ interior design
techne.com.au

photography: Tom Blachford
pp. 20–21
p. 232

That's mine
thatsmine.dk

p. 126 bottom

This Modern Life
thismodernlife.co.uk

interior design: Suzanne Harmar
photography: Andrew Hingston
p. 136–137
p. 178 top

TORAFU ARCHITECTS
torafu.com

p. 124 top
p. 127 top
p. 141 bottom
pp. 154–155

uuio
shop.uuio.de

photography: Matthias Oertel
p. 173
pp. 234–235

Julia von Werz
juliavonwerz.com

interior design: Julia von Werz
photography: Tom Mannion
pp. 28–29

Jennifer Yamsek

photography: Jennifer Yamsek
pp. 60–63